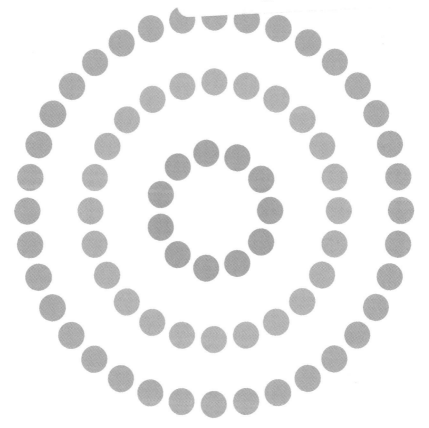

WHOLE-LIFE GENEROSITY
DEVOTIONAL

Living in Relationship, Gratitude, and Release

Skye Jethani

GENEROUSCHURCH

Published by GenerousChurch

 GENEROUSCHURCH

ISBN: 978-0-9981210-3-1

Cover Design: Michael Sean Allen
Editor and Interior Design: James Armstrong

Want to keep growing in generosity?
www.GenerousChurch.com

Printed in the U.S.A.

18 19 20 21 – 10 9 8 7 6 5 4 3 2 1
1st Printing

Contents

Week 4: Living with Generosity

Week 1

Living with God

Day 1 — What God Really Wants

*So God created man in his own image, in the image of God
he created him; male and female he created them.*

Genesis 1:27

EVERY RELIGION seeks to answer the question, "Why are
we here?" Unfortunately, some Christians have unknowingly
accepted a pagan vision of life that masquerades as a
Christian one, and the result is a false understanding of our
purpose, and this leads to a warped vision of generosity
as well. So, let's begin to set things right with a simple but
essential biblical truth—God does not need you.

Almost every ancient creation myth says that humans were
created to serve the gods. We were needed to build the
gods' temples, to provide food to the gods through our
sacrifices and to appease the gods' anger with our prayers
and worship. Pagan mythologies said our purpose was to be
the gods' slaves.

This pagan vision of life is turned upside down by what
God reveals about Himself in the Bible. Unlike the gods of
Babylon, Egypt or Rome, the God of Israel did not need to be
fed, clothed or housed by people. "If I were hungry, I would
not tell you," He said, "for the world and its fullness are mine"
(Psalm 50:12). And the Bible is clear that God does not live
in a temple built by people but has made the whole universe
His dwelling place (see Isaiah 66:1). In other words, Israel's
God did not need people. He does not need your service,
offerings or your generosity.

That explains why the story of creation in Genesis, unlike
pagan creation stories, does not depict humans as God's

servants but as His representatives. He made the man and woman in His image and gave them dominion over the earth (see Genesis 1:28-29). That means people were made to rule the earth with God—in relationship with Him and under His authority. And we were created to rule the earth like God—in a manner that reflected His own character and generosity.

If we are to begin the journey toward Whole-Life Generosity, we must abandon the myth that God needs our service or gifts. The consistent message of Scripture is that God does not need you, and any god that requires human help or gifts is not a god worthy of our worship. Instead, the Bible says God wants you. He desires to live with you, and through you to reveal His goodness to the world.

>> Reflect on how you have thought about generosity in the past. What has your view of generosity assumed about your relationship with God?

Reflection Notes

Day 2   Welcome to the Party

"Just as you, Father, are in me, and I in you,
[I ask] that they also may be in us."
John 17:21

A FEW YEARS AGO I was invited to a private reception at the Baseball Hall of Fame in Cooperstown, New York. It was a delightful but surreal experience mingling with the greatest athletes to ever play the game, especially because I did not know who most of them were. The other guests were intimately connected to Major League Baseball or at least immersed in the game's history. But not me. I'm not a baseball fan. As the son of an immigrant, I did not grow up playing or watching America's pastime. So, why was I there? It turns out my wife's great-great-grandfather was one of the early superstars of professional baseball, and our whole family was invited in his honor.

Entering into a relationship with Jesus is a bit like being invited to someone else's party; one that started long before you showed up. Some people mistakenly believe that before creating the world God was lonely, like a party host with no guests. So, God made people in order to have someone to love—objects for His affection and guests for His celebration. This view implies that God created us to fill some deficiency in His love or incompleteness in His being. This is silly, of course.

The Scriptures reveal a very different picture—an eternal, divine party of unimaginable love and joy that existed long before humans arrived on the scene. Although it is hard to grasp, the Bible speaks of God living in relationship with Himself. He is a community; a party of three and yet eternally one. Scripture gives us a stunning, and admittedly mind-twisting vision of one God eternally existing in three persons—God the Father, God the Son and God the Spirit. A full exploration of the doctrine of the Trinity is more than we can do in this devotional, but it is so foundational to our understanding of the Christian life that we cannot ignore it either.

The Christian belief in the Trinity means that God did not need to create us in order to express or receive love. Instead, He created us—and all things—from the overflow of the love shared between the Father, Son and Spirit. This is what separates the Christian vision of God from all others. We believe that relationship is central to God's being and central to our life with Him, and that has important implications for how we see ourselves and the source of our generosity.

If God did not create us because He needed to be loved or worshiped, then we can only conclude God created and redeemed us because He wanted us to share in the love that has been enjoyed between Father, Son and Spirit since before the world began. This helps us understand Jesus' prayer: "Just as you, Father, are in me, and I in you, [I ask] that they also may be in us" (John 17:21). Jesus invites us to share in the life and love of the Trinity. He wants us to join God's party and live in perpetual communion with Him.

Just as God created us from the overflow of love experienced within the Trinity, our generosity is also to be the overflow of the love experienced in our relationship with God.

>> In the past, would you say your acts of generosity were rooted more in a sense of obligation or in the overflow of your relationship with God?

Reflection Notes

Day 3 — Love Comes First

And behold, a voice from heaven said, "This is my beloved
Son, with whom I am well pleased."
Matthew 3:17

I ONCE SAW a bumper sticker that said: "JESUS LOVES YOU." Beneath it in a smaller font was added: "Then again, He loves everybody." While meant to be humorous, the sticker highlights an interesting dilemma. We want to be impressed and even overwhelmed by God's love for us. It should inspire our worship and provoke our obedience, but can we still be motivated by His love if it is indiscriminate? If every player gets a trophy, is mine still special? If God loves everyone, am I still special?

That question reveals a subtle error in our thinking. If we are claiming God's love as a way to elevate our value above that of others, then we have misunderstood the nature of divine love. Throughout the Bible we find God selecting people not because they are worthy of His love, but precisely because they are not. The fact that God loves a sinner like me makes Him special, it does not make me superior.

We fail to grasp this because the world has shaped us to think all love is conditional; that it must be earned. Therefore, when we hear, "God loves you," our inclination is to believe it's because we are more deserving than others. God's love, however, is unlike the world's.

Consider the Father's love for Jesus. At the moment of His baptism in the Jordan River, the voice of the Father spoke from heaven saying, "This is my beloved Son with whom I am well pleased." The Father's love for Jesus may not surprise you, but the timing of His declaration should. The Father said He was pleased with the Son before Jesus ever preached a sermon, before He performed any miracles, before He called a disciple or confronted a Pharisee, before He overcame the temptations of the devil, before He endured the humiliation of the Romans or the suffering of the cross. At that time Jesus had not yet completed any of His messianic calling. The Father declared Jesus' identity as His beloved before He had accomplished anything. The Father's love came first, not the Son's obedience.

Like Jesus, God's love for you is unconditional; you cannot earn it. We have already explored how God does not need your sacrifices or service, and He does not require your worship or devotion. That also means you cannot deserve or demand His love. It is a gift, generously and lavishly offered and totally undeserved. And far from elevating you above others, knowing God's love ought to amaze and humble you.

Ultimately we do not obey our heavenly Father or practice generosity so that He will call us His beloved. It is precisely the opposite. He has already declared you to be His beloved child, and when the miracle of that unconditional love saturates into your being, it will propel you to obey, serve and give. God's love comes first.

>> What are ways you tried to earn God's love in the past? How is this conditional vision of His love evident in the way some people practice generosity?

Reflection Notes

Day 4 — What to Use & What to Enjoy

"Son, you are always with me, and all that is mine is yours."
Luke 15:31

G. K. CHESTERTON ONCE SAID, "All evil comes from enjoying what we ought to use and using what we ought to enjoy." As we've already seen, God has created us to live in a perpetual, loving relationship with Himself. We were made to be loved and not merely used. The same is true about God, but our sinful tendency is to pursue God for His gifts rather than seek God Himself. The Bible calls this instinct to put the Creator's gifts ahead of the Creator Himself idolatry. Idolatry and its terrible effects appear all over the Scriptures. Jesus' story of the lost sons is one of those places, although it carries an important twist.

Jesus' parable is about two sons who were both fixated upon their father's property. The younger son wanted it to bankroll his selfish, immoral desires. The older son wanted it to elevate his status and reputation. The younger son was impatient and disrespectful. He confronted his father and demanded his half of the estate immediately. The older son, by contrast, worked hard and obeyed his father's instructions, seeking to earn his reward patiently. Despite their different tactics, it's important to recognize that both sons were so focused on their father's property that they overlooked the value of the father himself. They both wanted to use their father to enjoy his wealth.

At the end of the story the father finally reveals their foolishness. "Son," he said to his eldest, "you are always with me, and all that is mine is yours." His children chased after the father's property forgetting that they already possessed it. They displayed what all idolaters suffer from—misplaced desire. The sons wanted to use their father to gain the enjoyment of his wealth. Instead they should have used the wealth of their household to enjoy their relationship with their father. The father modeled the proper ordering of desire when he used his wealth to throw a party to celebrate the return of his younger son. Wealth is to be used. People are to be enjoyed.

We often make the same mistake as the sons. We chase after the gifts of God believing that in them we will find joy, peace, power and significance—all the while we forget that in Christ we have already been promised all things. How foolish to spend our lives chasing what we have already been given! Instead, we should seek after the One in whom our joy will be complete and our deepest desires satisfied. The things of this world are to be used and not worshiped, and our heavenly Father is to be worshiped and not used.

>> Share a story about a time when you were more fixated upon receiving something from God rather than pursuing a life with Him. How is this subtle form of idolatry encouraged even within Christian communities?

Reflection Notes

Day 5 — You Are Not Defined by Desires

*Man does not live by bread alone, but man lives by every
word that comes from the mouth of the Lord.*
Deuteronomy 8:3

JESUS HAD BEEN FASTING in the desert for 40 days. He
was understandably hungry, so the enemy presented to Him
a very practical and relevant idea. "If you are the Son of God,
tell this stone to become bread" (Luke 4:3 NAS). The enemy
was not saying that Jesus should prove His identity as God's
Son by turning stone into bread, although that is often how
we misread the story. The enemy was saying, "If you are
God's Son then you have every right to satisfy your desires.
You don't have to deny yourself or be hungry. Go ahead,
make some bread and eat. You're entitled to it."

Of course Jesus was God's Son, but He rejected this
invitation to satisfy His natural desire for food. Instead He
quoted Scripture, "It is written, man shall not live by bread
alone, but by every word that proceeds from the mouth
of God" (Matthew 4:4). Jesus understood that life is not
ultimately sustained by what we eat, but by God's will. True
life is to be found in Him and not merely by consuming His
gifts.

The temptation Jesus faced in the wilderness is one we
face every day. According to The New York Times, each
American is exposed to 3,500 desire-inducing ads a day,
each one promising us the life we've always wanted is just
one purchase away. Rodney Clapp says, "The consumer is
schooled in insatiability. He or she is never to be satisfied—
at least not for long. The consumer is tutored that people

basically consist of unmet needs that can only be appeased by commodified goods and experiences."

The world, like Jesus' enemy, tells us that we are defined by our desires, and the purpose of life is to satisfy them. To be fair, not every desire is ungodly or even unhealthy. There is nothing immoral about desiring food as Jesus did in the wilderness. The problem is that we have elevated desires to the status of rights and the thought that a desire should go unfulfilled, even temporarily, or that we should willingly deny ourselves in order to generously bless others, is utterly inconceivable to most people today. To deny ourselves a desire, we are told, is to deny our very identity and purpose! We have made our desires, rather than our Creator, the goal of life. And in this consumeristic soil, generosity is nearly impossible to cultivate.

That is why, more than ever, we need to hear the wisdom of Jesus: We do not live by bread alone. We are more than our desires, and the purpose of life is more than satisfying our natural longings however legitimate they may be. True life flows from the Living God, and our deepest longings are ultimately only satisfied in union with Him.

Real generosity will only be cultivated in our lives when we see God Himself, rather than material things, as the source of our life and well-being.

>> Rather than fasting from food as Jesus did in the wilderness, consider a media fast—a time to disconnect from all of the screens that bombard you with advertisements each day. Use the media fast to detox your soul and rediscover that you are more than a bundle of unmet desires.

Reflection Notes

Day 6 — A Prayer Life or a Praying Life

*Rejoice always, pray without ceasing, give thanks
in all circumstances; for this is the will of God in
Christ Jesus for you.*
1 Thessalonians 5:16-18

WHY DO WE STRUGGLE so much with prayer? I
am convinced that much of the burden comes from
misunderstanding the purpose of prayer. If we believe that
God exists to be used, that He is the means we employ to
get what we need or want, then prayer is a necessary chore
when life isn't going the way we desire. On the other hand, in
seasons of ease and contentment, prayer feels unnecessary
and is little more than a distraction forced upon our already
busy lives.

Dallas Willard offers a different perspective based on a more
integrated vision of life: "Don't seek to develop a prayer life,"
he said, "seek a praying life. A 'prayer life' is a segmented
time for prayer. You'll end feeling guilty that you don't spend
more time in prayer. Eventually you'll probably feel defeated
and give up. A 'praying life' is a life that is saturated with
prayerfulness—you seek to do all that you do with the Lord."

There's certainly nothing wrong with setting aside time for
prayer, but that is not the goal we are called to. Instead, if
we understand prayer to be how we relate with God and not
merely how we use Him, then it makes sense to integrate
our communion with God into all that we do and into every
moment of our day. Dallas Willard goes on: "Prayer is talking
with God about what we're thinking and doing together; it
is co-laboring with God to accomplish the good purposes of
His kingdom."

This life with God approach to prayer was demonstrated by Billy Graham in 1982 before an interview on The Today Show. When Graham arrived at the studio in New York, one of the program's producers informed his assistant that a private room had been set aside for the reverend to pray before the broadcast. The assistant thanked the producer for the thoughtful gesture but told him Mr. Graham would not need the room. The producer was a surprised that a world-famous Christian leader would not wish to pray before being interviewed on live national television.

Graham's assistant responded, "Mr. Graham started praying when he got up this morning, he prayed while eating breakfast, he prayed on the way over in the car, and he'll probably be praying all the way through the interview."

Before addressing how often you pray, or what you pray, take time to reflect upon why you pray. Are you trying to carve out a "prayer life" within your busy schedule, or are you cultivating a "praying life" of ceaseless communion with God? Is prayer how you try to use God, or how you seek to live with him?

>> The foundation of Whole-Life Generosity is our communion with God and experiencing His love. Discuss with others how you can begin to integrate an awareness of God's presence with you throughout your day.

Reflection Notes

Day 7   Worship Is Beautiful, Not Practical

One thing have I asked of the Lord, that will I seek after: that I may dwell in the house of the Lord all the days of my life, to gaze upon the beauty of the Lord.

Psalm 27:4

OUR CULTURE HAS FORMED US to think about nearly everything transactionally. Is what I will get equal to or greater than what I am being asked to give? This mindset even shapes how we think about worship. If I sacrifice my Sunday morning, what will I receive in exchange? Will the sermon be inspiring or at least helpful? Will the music be invigorating? Will my kids learn something useful if I go through the pain of getting them up and ready? Will God bless me if I give Him my morning?

But what if we're wrong? What if God did not intend for worship to be practical? What if worship is not transactional? King David, who led ancient Israel in worship as well as in battle, also wrote many of the songs they used to praise God. In Psalm 27, David reveals a very different motivation for worship. Rather than hoping for a return for his investment of time and effort in praising God, David says that all he wants is "to gaze upon the beauty of the Lord." David did not view worship as a transaction, but as infatuation.

Jesus affirmed this impractical understanding of worship shortly before His death. While reclining at a table, a woman poured a very expensive flask of oil upon His feet. When His disciples saw this they were outraged. Like many people today, they could only see through the lens of practicality. "This ointment could have been sold for more than three hundred denarii and given to the poor," they said, rebuking the woman.

"Leave her alone," Jesus shot back at them. "Why do you trouble her? She has done a beautiful thing to me" (Mark 14:5-6).

The disciples were thinking about a transaction. What could the ointment be exchanged for? Jesus, by contrast, was blessed by the woman's infatuation—her impractical and beautiful act of devotion. The disciples saw the spilled oil as a lost opportunity. To them the oil was only a commodity to be utilized and exchanged for a measurable outcome. What they interpreted as a waste, however, Jesus saw as priceless. He recognized the spilled oil as an outpouring of worship.

True worship can never be wasteful because it seeks no return on investment. True worship is never a transaction. It is always a gift—an extravagant, wasteful gift. In a word, true worship is generously giving to God and desiring only God in return.

>> As you reflect on David's song and the woman at Jesus' feet, consider how their vision of God informed their worship. How do you see God, and how does your understanding of Him inform the way you worship?

Reflection Notes

Week 2

Living with God

Day 8 — What Makes God Happy?

"Fear not, little flock, for it is your Father's good pleasure to give you the kingdom."
Luke 12:32

THIS WEEK WE'RE EXPLORING what it means to live with gratitude, why giving thanks to God with a joyful heart is so important. To start, we need to look more closely at God's heart and what makes Him joyful. We may think of God as powerful, or merciful or loving, but have you considered that God, in His nature, is happy? In Luke 12, Jesus offers us a glimpse into the joyful heart of our heavenly Father.

After listing common fears we all experience, Jesus tells His followers to abandon their worry. Your Father knows what you need, Jesus assures His followers, and He'll provide it. What Jesus says next was life-changing for me: "Fear not, little flock, for it is your Father's good pleasure to give you the kingdom."

There is such tenderness in these words. Jesus calls us His little flock. He is our Good Shepherd who cares for us, knows our name, and guides us through the dark and dangerous places to safe pastures where all of our needs will be met. Because He is our Shepherd, we do not have to live in fear.

It gets even better. He says it is the Father's good pleasure to give us the kingdom. Another translation says the Father "chooses gladly" to give it. Some mistakenly think "the kingdom" refers to heaven or some celestial afterlife, but Jesus uses "the kingdom" to speak of God's own presence. It is the domain where He reigns and where His will is always done. To be in God's kingdom is to be united with God Himself.

Jesus says that God doesn't give to us His presence and all of its accompanying blessings begrudgingly. We don't have to pry good things from His hands or cajole Him into being kind to us. Our heavenly Father delights over us, and it actually brings Him pleasure to give us the kingdom along with everything else that we need. Our heavenly Father wants us to know life with Him, and He welcomes us with a smile.

Is it possible that God receives more joy from us than we are capable of receiving from Him? And if providing for our needs brings the Creator of the universe pleasure, if it makes Him smile, what can possibly make us afraid?

Joy is infectious. Its energy is uncontainable; it overflows from one person to another. There is no one more joyful than our heavenly Father, and as we live in communion with Him, we will find ourselves carried along in the current of His pleasure. If you desire to live a life of joyful gratitude, it begins by recognizing God's joy over you.

>> Take time to consider what brings you great joy. Can you imagine God feeling that way about caring for you? What false ideas about God's character keep you from expressing thanks to Him?

Reflection Notes

Day 9 Gratitude Connects Sunday to Monday

And whatever you do, in word and deed, do everything in the name of the Lord Jesus, giving thanks to God the Father through him.
Colossians 3:17

CULTIVATING A LIFE WITH GOD, as we explored last week, is the foundation of Whole-Life Generosity. This daily communion is the engine that generates the power in the Christian's life—including the power to give ourselves selflessly to bless others. Power alone, however, is not enough. A car may have a state of the art engine that produces enough horsepower to launch a space shuttle, but if that power cannot get to the tires, the car is useless.

Similarly, some are inclined to develop a deep, personal connection with God in prayer, worship and solitude. Where we struggle, however, is activating this private faith once we leave the sanctuary. Some have talked about the "Sunday to Monday gap." The faith we celebrate and affirm at church on Sunday often has little influence in the grind of daily reality we experience Monday through Saturday. For our faith to be real, for it to be truly meaningful, it must be alive in the hustle and bustle of the world. What is the point of having a car that cannot leave the garage? What is the point of having a faith that cannot leave the church?

That's the role of gratitude. It activates our life with God in the world and bridges Sunday's worship with Monday's work. Gratitude is the transmission that connects the engine to the tires. Ann Voskamp says, "Giving thanks...is the way we practice the presence of God, stay present to His presence, and it is always a practice of the eyes. We don't have to change what we see. Only the way we see."

Her point is important. Unlike our time in the sanctuary, it is all too easy to lose sight of God's presence when we are engaged in the messy, often mundane realities of the world. Practicing gratitude consistently—even for the messy and mundane things of life—is how we stay connected to God and invite His power and presence into everything we do. In the process, it changes the way we see things. Gratitude gives us the eyes to recognize God's presence and grace in the most unusual and unexpected places.

This is why the Apostle Paul calls us to give thanks in "whatever you do, in word and deed." Without practicing gratitude we will lose sight of God, and our faith will become a sacred but isolated part of our life. It won't overflow into the real world we inhabit.

>> In order to practice thankfulness more consistently throughout your week, consider using a simple reminder to give God thanks. For example, every time you look at a clock or pass through a doorway—offer a silent prayer of thanksgiving. Others find keeping a thanksgiving journal transformative. Each day think of three things you are thankful for. Offer this time as a prayer to God.

Reflection Notes

Day 10 | A God of Abundance

"At twilight you shall eat meat, and in the morning you shall be filled with bread. Then you shall know that I am the Lord your God."

Exodus 16:12

THOSE WHO DISCOVER A LIFE with God, who draw into intimate communion with Him, will come to see the world very differently. Rather than a place of scarcity and fear, a life with God opens our eyes to recognize a world of abundance that leads to gratitude.

Consider the story of God's people in Exodus. Pharaoh, the king of Egypt, represented the view of scarcity. The Egyptians were threatened by the growth of the Hebrews, so to protect their own power and limited resources they persecuted the Hebrews and killed their children. A belief in scarcity—that there isn't enough for everyone to flourish—led Pharaoh to violence, injustice and greed.

God's people, on the other hand, experienced a world of abundance. Every day the Lord provided them with meat and bread in the wilderness, and water miraculously flowed from rocks in the desert. God's people always had enough without having to use greed or injustice to ensure their survival. Assured of God's provision, they were called to put aside the ways of Egypt and instead seek justice, love kindness and walk humbly with God.

In the Sermon on the Mount, Jesus makes the same contrast between the myth of the world's scarcity and the reality of abundance in God's kingdom. If we live in constant fear of not having enough, like Pharaoh, it will lead us to greed and injustice in the name of self-preservation, and it will short-circuit our ability to live with gratitude or practice generosity. Instead, we will be consumed with worry about not having enough for ourselves.

If, however, we believe Jesus' words and trust that with God there is always an abundance, then we can be set free from a self-centered posture to truly love others. We can view them with compassion rather than as competition. We can give, and serve and sacrifice knowing that our needs will be provided for by our heavenly Father, because with Him there is always more than enough. And rather than always worrying about having enough for the future, we are set free to be grateful for God's provision for today.

>> How do you see the world? Do you believe in the myth of scarcity, or have you been liberated by the abundance of God's kingdom? If you had absolute assurance that you would always have enough, how would your practice of generosity change?

Reflection Notes

Day 11 | Pure Thanksgiving

Then one of them, when he saw that he was healed, turned back, praising God with a loud voice; and he fell on his face at Jesus' feet, giving him thanks.

Luke 17:15-16

WHY DO WE GIVE THANKS? On the surface, gratitude is a natural response to good favor. When life is good and we are blessed, our instinct is to be thankful. For religious people, however, thanksgiving is often practiced with another, concealed agenda. Beneath the surface, sometimes even hidden from our own awareness, is a more manipulative motive: If I offer these prayers, if I give these sacrifices and if I show my gratitude for past blessings, then perhaps God will bless me again.

Some give thanks to God for the same reason a person gives a generous gratuity at a restaurant they frequent—to ensure the same positive service the next time they call upon God for help. In this scenario, gratitude is predicated upon a consumeristic or superstitious vision of God.

There is another, purer form of thanksgiving which seeks nothing in return. We see this displayed in Luke 17. While passing through a village, ten lepers cried out to Jesus for mercy. He instructed the lepers to present themselves to the temple priests, and on their way all ten were healed. One, however, returned to Jesus, fell on his face, and gave Him thanks.

Why didn't the other nine return and offer their gratitude as well? Most likely because they had already received what they desired; they were already healed and there was nothing more to be gained by giving thanks to Jesus.

For the nine, and for many of us, gratitude is a transactional practice. We worship, praise and express gratitude because we're expecting something in return, and when no return is possible, or no further blessing is desired, we see no need to offer our thanks to God.

For the one leper who returned, however, giving thanks was pure. He thanked Jesus because he was overwhelmed with gratitude not just for his healing, but to the One who healed him. Pure thanksgiving is possible when we focus on the source of our blessings rather than merely the blessings themselves.

>> Reflect upon a time when someone expressed pure gratitude to you without any agenda. How did it make you feel? Would you describe your gratitude toward God as pure or laced with hidden motives?

Reflection Notes

Day 12 | Fear Is the Enemy of Gratitude

Keep your life free from love of money...for he has said,
"I will never leave you nor forsake you."
Hebrews 13:5

THE MOST REPEATED COMMANDS in the Bible are not
warnings or restrictions. They are calls to "praise the Lord"
and "do not be afraid." These commands take different forms
such as "give thanks," "rejoice," and "fear not" throughout
Scripture, but the emphasis remains the same—God's desire
is for us to be full of joy and gratitude, but He knows that fear
is always lurking and ready to hijack our souls. Fear is the
enemy of gratitude.

Biology tells us that when a creature is afraid, it will respond
in two ways—fight or flight. It will either try to overpower the
threat or escape from it. Both responses are ways of seeking
control over a dangerous situation. People are no different.
When we are afraid, we try to gain control over the world in
order to feel safe again. This leads to two problems.

First, fear drives us to take control rather than trust God. If we
believe it's our strength and wisdom that is keeping us safe,
what need is there for gratitude toward God? This posture of
self-reliance is all too common today and may explain why
fewer people incorporate worship and thanksgiving to the
Lord as regular practices.

Second, fear prevents us from recognizing that control is
an illusion. No amount of control will ever be enough to
guarantee our safety, and no degree of control will fully
take away our fears. Whatever solace we may gain from our
attempts at control may be nothing more than a placebo. We

may be fooling ourselves into thinking we are safe when we are not.

Jesus illustrated the illusion of control with a story about a man with great wealth and storehouses of grain. The man said to himself, "You have ample goods laid up for many years; relax, eat, drink, be merry." But God called the man a fool. "This night your soul is required of you, and the things you have prepared, whose will they be?" (Luke 12:19-20). Jesus revealed that the sense of security we gain from wealth is an illusion.

Our desire for safety is not wrong, it is merely misplaced. We look to protect ourselves from the uncertainty of this world by seeking control—often by accumulating wealth—but the peace we are longing for cannot be found in money. This is why the writer of Hebrews connects a life freed from a love of money with the promise of God to never leave us nor forsake us. Our fearful instinct is to find safety in wealth rather than in Christ. Sin tells us to pursue control rather than gratitude.

If we truly believe that God is with us and that He will never leave us, then what can make us afraid? When we come to recognize the illusion of control and embrace the promise of God's never-ending presence and care, we unlock the door to a life of joyful gratitude.

>> Share a time when you felt the least amount of control. How did that realization affect your faith? What fears are currently blocking your ability to express gratitude to God?

_____

_____

_____

_____

Reflection Notes

Day 13   Compare and Despair

Giving thanks always and for everything to God the Father in the name of our Lord Jesus Christ.

Ephesians 5:20

THE APOSTLE PAUL TELLS US to "give thanks always." This command sounds like an exaggeration, but I don't think it is. Paul understood something important about our sinful nature—giving thanks is the key to contentment. Likewise, when we stop practicing gratitude, we will grow increasingly discontent and irritable. We will inevitably begin comparing our circumstances to others' rather than welcoming our circumstances as the place we are called to discover God's presence with us.

Not long ago a stunning new car pulled up beside me at a stop light—a marvel of engineering and design. I noted its aerodynamic shape evident even in the brilliant design of its door handles. What began as admiration, however, soon deteriorated as my gaze drifted to the stains and duct tape marking the interior of my ten-year-old Volkswagen.

"Compare and despair," is a phrase we often use in our home. It's our way of reminding the kids, and one another, that the grass always looks greener on the other side of the fence, but it still needs to be mowed. Fixating on what others have, and what we do not, never leads to happiness. This temptation has only grown stronger with the advent of social media and smartphones. These devices bombard us with the constant invitation to compare the inglorious reality of our lives with the carefully curated images and posts of others. This helps explain why researchers have discovered a correlation between increased time on social media and higher rates of depression. Social media is a "compare and despair" engine.

Of course the dangers of comparing are not limited to our phones. When I was simply admiring the design of the other car next to me at the stoplight, I felt no discontent, but when I compared it to my own vehicle, things quickly went downhill. What is the solution? How do we get off the treadmill of discontent? How do we not constantly compare our circumstances to others' when everywhere we look, every form of media we engage and virtually everything in our consumer society is designed to make us discontent?

I've found nothing dissipates discontent better than practicing thankfulness—even when we do not feel like it. At the stoplight it meant thanking God for what I do have—a functioning car that serves my needs—and even expressing gratefulness for the gifted people who created the incredible machine parked next to me.

Rather than simply turning my eyes away from the car—which isn't always possible when driving—I chose to look at it differently. Not as a possession to desire, but as a creation to admire. In the process I found my discontent evaporating. In its place came a sense of wonder at the ingenuity and creativity of humans. Surely we have been created in the image of a creative God, I thought.

Yes, a car provoked me to think of God. That is the power of practicing thankfulness. It can transform greed into gratitude and worry into worship. It can even move our hearts from a desire to possess to a posture of praise.

>> When do you feel most discontent or the temptation to compare and despair? What might you remove or limit in your life to foster a greater sense of contentment? (Maybe social media?) The next time you feel discontent, try to immediately shift your mind to thanks.

WHOLE-LIFE GENEROSITY DEVOTIONAL

Day 14   The Goal of Gratitude

Give thanks in all circumstances; for this is the
will of God in Christ Jesus for you.
1 Thessalonians 5:18

LIKE THE COMMANDS IN SCRIPTURE to love, forgive and
serve, the instruction to give thanks does not depend on
one's feelings. It is something we are called to do whether
we feel like it or not. In this way gratitude is a discipline. Like
any athletic or academic discipline, spiritual disciplines are
practices that help us reach a goal we could not otherwise
reach.

For example, as a boy I struggled so terribly with reading
that I was assigned to a special education class. My very
patient teacher, Mrs. Schwab, gave me reading exercises for
homework. I did not want to do those exercises after school;
I wanted to watch cartoons. The discipline of homework,
however, taught me to read, which I now do automatically
and even joyfully. The discipline of my reading exercises
equipped me to reach a goal I would never have reached on
my own. They trained and equipped me to live differently.

So, what is that goal behind the discipline of gratitude?
Giving thanks allows us to see the light of God in a world
often filled with shadows. It trains us to recognize hope amid
despair, to smile amid suffering, and to know the reality of
God's presence even when He seems distant. Simply put,
practicing gratitude teaches us how to walk in faith.

For example, the apostle James tells us to "count it all joy
when you face trials of various kinds," because through
such struggles good things will be produced in our life

and character. (See James 1:2-4.) In other words, when we practice gratitude even amid suffering, it helps us recognize that our present circumstances, which others may have intended for our harm, God intends for our good. He will redeem and use even our struggles to produce good things. The ability to gain this perspective comes when we practice the discipline of thanksgiving even when we do not feel like it.

When we stop giving thanks and instead allow our feelings of jealousy, despair or discontent to determine our actions, it becomes far more difficult to recognize the presence of God or the hope of His redemption. In this way gratitude is not only the outcome of faith but also its source.

>> Consider an area of your life in which you practice a discipline. What helps you stay committed to that discipline when you do not feel like engaging it? Similarly, what structures or accountability might help you practice the discipline of gratitude when you do not feel thankful?

Reflection Notes

Week 3

Living with Faith

Day 15   A City under Siege

There is no fear in love, but perfect love casts out fear.
1 John 4:18

MANY OF US HAVE BEEN TAUGHT that doubt is the opposite of faith, but this view assumes faith is the intellectual agreement with a set of ideas. Therefore, the opposite of faith must be to question, or doubt, those ideas. While faith certainly has an intellectual component, the Bible sees faith as more than agreement with a set of ideas. It means to put one's confidence or trust in something. For this reason, Scripture most often presents fear, not doubt, as the opposite of faith.

The medieval theologian, Thomas Aquinas, said that fear is a contracting impulse of the soul. It causes us to turn inward to focus only on ourselves. From this posture, we cannot love, give or serve others. "It drives compassion right out of our heart," he said. Aquinas compared a fearful person to a medieval city under siege. The resources and inhabitants from the surrounding country retreat into the city and barricade themselves behind its walls. No one else is allowed in and nothing is given out. Survival is the only objective.

When we are afraid, it is all too easy to become self-absorbed and justify our lack of generosity. We turn inward and can only think of ourselves, and from this posture compassion and love toward others becomes impossible. Fear prevents us from seeing beyond our own needs.

Putting our faith in Jesus, however, ends the siege and breaks down the wall. Faith means trusting that God loves me and will let no ultimate harm come to me. His love for us, and

His power to redeem us, was proven when He sent His own Son to die in order to reconcile us to Himself. As Paul says in Romans 8:31-32, "If God is for us, who can be against us? He who did not spare his own Son but gave him up for us all, how will he not also with him graciously give us all things?"

In the same chapter, Paul goes on to express our perfect safety in God's hands: "I am sure that neither death nor life, nor angels nor rulers, nor things present nor things to come, nor powers, nor height nor depth, nor anything else in all creation, will be able to separate us from the love of God in Christ Jesus our Lord" (Romans 8:38-39).

When we come to recognize and trust God's incomprehensible love for us, we discover the courage to abandon our fears. It gives us the courage to break down the walls of selfishness and open our hearts to others. This trust is what empowered Peter to step out of the boat and walk with Jesus on the sea. This trust is what empowered Paul to face imprisonment, beatings and persecution without despair. And this trust is what opens our hearts to give ourselves generously to others.

>> Discuss how you think nonbelievers view Christians. Do they view us as loving, generous, self-sacrificial people like Jesus? If not, what role do you think fear has in the posture Christians take toward those outside the faith?

Reflection Notes

Day 16 | Trust the Catcher

*Be strong and courageous. Do not fear or be in dread
of them, for it is the Lord your God who goes with you.
He will not leave you or forsake you.*

Deuteronomy 31:6

HENRI NOUWEN, A DUTCH PRIEST, professor, and author,
came to more clearly understand the nature of faith through
the Flying Rodleighs, a trapeze troupe from South Africa.
Nouwen noticed that while everyone is fixated upon the
flyer's aerial acrobatics, they are missing the true star of the
performance. The audience forgets that the flyer's amazing
act is only possible because he knows he will be safely
caught. Everything depends upon the other trapeze artist—
the catcher. Nouwen wrote:

> "If we are to take risks, to be free, in the air, in life, we
> have to know there's a catcher. We have to know that
> when we come down from it all, we're going to be
> caught, we're going to be safe. The great hero is the
> least visible. Trust the catcher."

Faith is the opposite of seeking control. Faith is willfully
surrendering control and entrusting yourself into the hands
of God. It is letting go and trusting that you will be caught.
Faith is "the assurance of things hoped for, the conviction of
things not seen" (Hebrews 11:1). It is believing the promise that
no matter what happens, God will not let you fall.

The assurance that we will be caught by God is what makes
obeying Him possible, and without this assurance we will
see many of Jesus' commands as either impossible or
irresponsible. Consider a few of His instructions from The

Sermon on the Mount (Matthew 5-7): Do not fight back, forgive everyone, do not judge, do not worry, give to whoever asks you, pray for and love your enemies. From the world's perspective these are risky, even foolish teachings to follow. That may explain why so few people, including Christians, seem to take them seriously. Unlimited forgiveness, generosity and love are not how to protect yourself or how get ahead in a dangerous world. In fact, Jesus lived this way and it landed him on a Roman cross.

But Jesus' life of obedience to God proves Henri Nouwen's point about trusting the Catcher. The world did the worst thing possible to Jesus, and His heavenly Father still caught Him. Jesus was not abandoned to the grave, but God raised Him up and "bestowed on him the name that is above every name" (Philippians 2:9). Safety is the prerequisite of obedience, including obeying Jesus' call to be generous.

>> When was the last time you had the opportunity to act generously but declined? Can you identify what fear held you back? If you were certain God would "catch" you, how would you have acted differently?

Reflection Notes

Day 17 Moving toward Maturity

"Fear not, for I have redeemed you; I have called you by name, you are mine. When you pass through the waters, I will be with you; and through the rivers, they shall not overwhelm you."

Isaiah 43:1-2

FOR MANY OF US, FAITH WAS EASY as children but has become far more difficult to sustain as adults. The problem, at least in part, is that we try to carry our childish faith into adulthood and find it inadequate.

Imagine if you stopped learning math in second grade or never attempted to read anything more than picture books. As an adult, you'd quickly find your math and reading skills inadequate for real life in the larger world. Yet this is precisely what many of us do with faith. We assume a childish understanding of God will be sufficient to meet adult challenges. When it isn't, we assign the blame to God or faith itself rather than our failure to nurture our faith toward maturity.

The Scottish philosopher John MacMurray contrasts two kinds of faith. The first, which he calls "illusory religion," is how many children think about God. He describes it this way: "Fear not; trust in God and He will see that none of the things you fear will happen to you." Another word for this is superstition—just follow the rules and rituals you'll be OK. This is the sort of faith that is sure to fail us in adulthood when all kinds of trials and pains will assail us.

The other kind of faith, what MacMurray calls "real religion," is nuanced, mature and biblical. This more adult faith says:

"Fear not; the things you are afraid of are quite likely to happen to you, but they are nothing to be afraid of." A person with this perspective does not follow every superstition promising deliverance from all of life's challenges. Instead, she understands that troubles are very likely to come, but it is precisely amid those challenges that we discover God is with us. And while troubles are unavoidable in this world, our ultimate security is not at risk. As Jesus said, "In the world you will have tribulation. But take heart; I have overcome the world" (John 16:33).

MacMurray's two models of faith capture the difference between adolescent and adult faith. One tries to use God to avoid reality and escape pain. The other accepts reality and embraces pain knowing that God will meet us in the midst of it.

>> Sometimes being generous is painful. An immature faith focused on avoiding discomfort is not sufficient for Whole-Life Generosity. Can you think of a time when being generous, in any way, was uncomfortable for you? Why did you do it? What blessing came from pursing generosity ahead of comfort?

Reflection Notes

Day 18 When God Says "No"

"If you then, who are evil, know how to give good gifts to your children, how much more will your Father who is in heaven give good things to those who ask him!"

Matthew 7:11

Jesus said that God hears our prayers with the ears of a loving Father who gives good things to His children. With this image of God in mind, we are to ask for what we need and desire. This has led some to incorrectly think God will grant whatever we ask. No caring parent—earthly or heavenly— always says "yes" to their child. Sometimes saying "no" is actually proof of their love, not its absence.

On a trip to New Delhi with my father many years ago, we were approached by a young boy on the street. He was rail thin, virtually naked, and his legs were stiff and contorted like a wire hanger twisted upon itself. He waddled on his hands and kneecaps over the broken pavement. The boy hounded us with his shouts. "One rupee, please! One rupee!" Finally, my father stopped.

"What do you want?" he asked.

"One rupee, sir," the boy said. My father laughed.

"How about I give you five rupees?" he said. The boy's countenance suddenly became defiant. He retracted his hand and sneered at us. He thought my father was joking; having a laugh at his expense. After all, no one would give five rupees when he only asked for one. The boy started shuffling away, mumbling curses under his breath. When he heard the jingle of the coins from my father's pocket, however, the boy stopped and looked back over his shoulder. My father was holding out a five-rupee coin and placed it in the boy's hand. Stunned, he didn't move or say a word.

This, I imagine, is how our heavenly Father sees us—as broken creatures in desperate need of His help, but rather than asking for what we truly need, rather than desiring what He is able and generously willing to give, we settle for lesser things. And when God graciously says "no" to our misled requests and instead offers us more, we reject Him. We turn away, cursing Him under our breath.

Always getting what we want is not evidence of a mature faith. In fact, it is precisely the opposite. A mature faith learns to trust God even when He says "no," believing His purposes are more loving and His grace more abounding that we can imagine. When our Lord says "no" to our desires, it is because He loves us too much to say "yes."

>> There are times when a commitment to love and generosity actually means saying "no" to another's request. Share a time when you benefited because you did not receive what you asked for. How should we evaluate which requests of us to grant and which to deny?

Reflection Notes

Day 19   Enough Faith for Today

*"Therefore do not be anxious, saying, 'What shall we eat?'
or 'What shall we drink?' or 'What shall we wear?'...your
heavenly Father knows that you need them all."*
Matthew 6:31-32

WHEN JESUS WAS TEACHING His disciples to pray, He told them to say, "Give us this day our daily bread." It's important to see that Jesus didn't instruct His followers to say, "Give us everything we'll need forever." Instead, He told them to request their daily bread. That means asking for enough for today. Jesus calls us to trust our heavenly Father to supply our needs for today, and then trust Him again tomorrow for tomorrow's needs.

This simple prayer shows that a life of faith is one of ongoing, unending, daily dependence. Faith is not like a divine immunization shot—one dose and you are covered for eternity. Faith is like food—like daily bread—that must be ingested regularly to nourish and sustain our life with God.

When we understand faith this way, it helps us recognize the sacredness of the present. The world tempts us with nostalgia for the past (a fixation on how good things used to be) or anxiety about the future (constant worry about what may or may not happen tomorrow). A life with God, however, cannot be lived in the past or in the future. It can only be experienced in the present. Today is the only place we may experience and trust God.

Recognizing the daily nature of faith provides an antidote to the worry and busyness that plagues so many of us. Has it ever occurred to you that Jesus never hurried? There is no record in the gospels of Jesus rushing or worrying. He trusted that His Father would provide for Him each day, and He taught this kind of faith to His followers. "You of little faith! Do not worry then, saying, 'What will we eat?' or 'What will we drink?' or 'What will we wear for clothing?' For the Gentiles eagerly seek all these things; for your heavenly Father knows that you need all these things...But seek first His kingdom and His righteousness, and all these things will be added to you. So do not worry about tomorrow; for tomorrow has enough trouble of its own" (Matthew 6:30-34 NAS).

When we live the kind of faith expressed in the Lord's Prayer, we learn to let go of our rushing; we learn to release our fear of not having enough. Instead we are set free to slow down, trust our Father and discover that true life is not found in what we eat, or drink, or wear, or drive.

What an incredible challenge for us. In the wealthiest, busiest culture that has ever existed, Jesus comes asking, Will you be content with enough for today? Will you slow down and trust God now? Will you release your worries and find true contentment in communion with God today?

>> Sometimes we can be overwhelmed by the needs in our world, and we feel incapable of giving everything needed. Practicing Whole-Life Generosity doesn't mean giving enough to end another's needs forever; sometimes it's simply meeting a need for today. What is something you can do to help another right now? A kind word? A small gift? A helping hand? How can you be someone else's daily bread from God?

Reflection Notes

Day 20 | Surrender All

*Trust in the Lord with all your heart, and do not
lean on your own understanding. In all your ways
acknowledge him, and he will make straight
your paths.*

Proverbs 3:5-6

To have faith means to trust. Taking my seat on an airplane,
for example, is an act of faith. I am trusting the pilots, the
air traffic controllers and the engineers and mechanics who
built and maintain the plane. I fly often and usually enjoy
the experience. In fact, I often find myself marveling at the
wonder of it all.

As a child, however, I was terrified of flying. I never would
have boarded an airplane had my parents not forced me.
Flying made me tense, I was hyper-sensitive to every sound
and bump, and I even became nauseous before ever leaving
the ground. I may have been on the plane, but I did not trust
the plane.

Similarly, having faith in God means trusting Him. Faith is
surrendering to His goodness, love and power. It means
releasing ourselves into His care. Like my childhood fear of
flying, however, it is possible to believe God exists, and even
know Him personally, but still not fully trust Him.

Consider the story of Jacob from Genesis 32. He was about
to be reunited with his brother, Esau, whom Jacob had
cheated out of his birthright. The night before the reunion,
Jacob was alone when the Lord appeared to him as a man
and wrestled with him. During the fight, Jacob said to the
Lord, "I will not let you go unless you bless me" (v. 26).

Afraid of Esau's vengeance, Jacob desperately wanted God's assurance of his safety.

Like Jacob, many of us struggle with God because we do not trust His goodness toward us. In our fear, we desperately try to maintain control and force blessings from God's hands.

After wrestling with God all night, Jacob was finally defeated when the Lord merely touched his hip and it went out of joint. By physically breaking Jacob, God was revealing his true condition. He forced Jacob, perhaps for the first time, to accept that he was not in control. Rather than demanding God's blessing, Jacob finally had to surrender to God's goodness and trust the Lord.

I finally began to overcome my fear of flying when, as a teenager, I realized that no amount of worrying could make me safe. I had no control; I was at the mercy of the pilots and airplane. After numerous long international flights, I finally learned to surrender. I learned to trust.

God's love and blessing cannot be demanded; it cannot be wrested from His hands. We have no status or strength to force God to do anything. We are not in control. Until we recognize and accept that fact, faith will be inaccessible to us. Faith is not merely agreeing that God exists, nor is it expecting God to obey our demands like a genie. Faith accepts that we have no ultimate control but instead surrenders all things to God's gracious care.

>> How eager are you to be generous? Do you only give of your time, resources or energy when someone wrestles it out of you? The next time someone asks you for something, as an experiment say "yes" immediately and record how the experience blessed you and the other person.

Reflection Notes

Day 21 | Seeing through Another's Eyes

*Let us consider how to stir up one another to love and
good works, not neglecting to meet together, as is the
habit of some, but encouraging one another.*

Hebrews 10:24-25

JOHN THE BAPTIST WAS LOCKED AWAY in a dungeon,
a prisoner of an evil and illegitimate king. In that terrible
place, John questioned Jesus' power and identity. He sent
his followers to Jesus with a question: "Are you the one, or
should we expect another?" (See Luke 7:20.) The question
revealed the depth of John's despair. After all, he had been
the first person to declare Jesus' identity as the Messiah, the
Lamb of God, and John had heard the voice of the Father
declare at Jesus' baptism, "This is my beloved Son."

Then John's circumstances took a dark turn. He could no
longer see Jesus' miracles or hear His teaching. As a result,
his faith in Jesus' identity was fading. John had fallen into the
shadowlands. The wickedness of King Herod's persecution
and the awfulness of his dungeon had blocked John's vision
of the Light. God had not abandoned John, nor had Jesus'
identity or mission changed—but from John's vantage point
he could see neither.

When Jesus heard John's question and understood his
despair, He sent friends back to John with a message.
"Go and tell John what you have seen and heard," Jesus
instructed them. "The blind receive their sight, the lame walk,
lepers are cleansed, and the deaf hear..." (Luke 7:22). Through
his friends, Jesus wanted John to see the light that was
hidden from his sight in Herod's prison and be encouraged.

John's experience in the shadows reminds us why a life of faith must be pursued in community. There will be times when sin and circumstances conspire to block our vision of God, when we fall into the shadowlands and question Jesus' presence and power. In those seasons, we need to see the light through the eyes of others—our sisters and brothers on higher ground, who can see the sun beyond our valley of tears.

This is precisely why Scripture tells us to meet together regularly. We need the encouragement of others if we are to persevere and mature in our faith. On any given Sunday, there will be some believers who are struggling to see God's presence and power. They are, like John, trapped in the world's dark dungeon. They need you, their sister or brother, to come alongside and tell how you have seen Jesus at work.

Before long, you may find the roles are reversed. You will be the one in a dungeon of doubt, and it will be the community that gathers to encourage your faith. John discovered what we also need to learn. Following Jesus take more than faith. It takes a community.

>> Invite each person to share whether they feel like they are in a season of shadow or light. Are they struggling to see God's goodness, or do they have something to share that will encourage others? Sharing our stories of God's goodness is another way of expressing Whole-Life Generosity.

Reflection Notes

Week 4

Living with Generosity

Day 22 | Fruit Happens

"Abide in me, and I in you. As the branch cannot bear fruit by itself, unless it abides in the vine, neither can you, unless you abide in me."

John 15:4

FOR THE FIRST THREE WEEKS we have been looking at generosity indirectly, which may seem odd in a devotional that is supposed to be about "Whole-Life Generosity." Why is that? That's a fair question, and the answer is all about fruit.

We live in a self-improvement culture that says whatever is undesirable or undeveloped in us can be changed with a combination of knowledge and willpower. You just need to read the right book, get into the right program or work the right system to become the person you want to be. We often transfer these assumptions into our life with God as well. Do you want to become a more generous person? Well, here's your three-step process. Now get to work!

According to Jesus, that's not how real transformation happens.

He often compared people to trees. The fruit a tree produces, He said, is determined by the identity of the tree. A good tree will produce good fruit; a bad tree will produce bad fruit (see Matthew 7:17). An apple tree cannot produce apricots, and a peach tree cannot make mangos. No amount of knowledge, willpower or effort will change a tree's fruit; it is inherent to the tree's identity. Fruit happens.

This is perplexing to those in a self-improvement culture. We read in the Bible that the fruit of the Spirit "is love, joy, peace,

WEEK 4: LIVING WITH GENEROSITY

patience, kindness, goodness, faithfulness, gentleness, self-control" (Galatians 5:22-23), and we immediately look for the program that will produce more of these qualities in our lives. Similarly, we assume generosity is gained by directly pursuing generosity. That may be true temporarily, but what we're after is a kind of generosity that permeates and marks our entire life. That requires more than just trying harder.

Good fruit, Jesus says, is not achieved by directly pursuing good fruit. Instead, it is the byproduct of pursuing a life rooted in God. Rather than focusing on our fruit, we should pay attention to our roots. We must become people rooted in God and thriving on His Spirit; then we will naturally, and even effortlessly, produce the good fruit of His kingdom. This is why Jesus said, "Abide in me, and I in you. As the branch cannot bear fruit by itself, unless it abides in the vine, neither can you, unless you abide in me." The Christian's role is to abide in Jesus, and the fruit will take care of itself.

That explains why this devotional has emphasized our communion with God through prayer, gratitude and faith before turning our attention to the direct practice of generosity. When we daily abide with Jesus, through faith and rooted in His love, generosity won't be a painful discipline requiring coercion. Instead, it will be the natural overflow of God's generosity toward us.

>> Share a time when you tried to directly transform the "fruit" of your life—when you tried through force of will to become more loving, patient, kind, generous, etc. What was that experience like? How effective was it?

Reflection Notes

Day 23 Connecting the Vertical & the Horizontal

"You shall love the Lord your God with all your heart...and your neighbor as yourself."
Luke 10:27

"What must I do to have eternal life?" That is the question an expert in the Scriptures asked Jesus. Being a wise teacher, Jesus put the question back to the man.

"What is written in the Law?" Jesus said.

"'Love the Lord your God with all your heart and with all your soul and with all your strength and with all your mind'; and, 'Love your neighbor as yourself.'"

"You are correct," Jesus said. "Do this and you will live." (See Luke 10:25-28.)

The man's answer echoed what Jesus Himself had taught on numerous occasions— eternal life with God is about more than loving God, because the way we show our love for God is by loving those around us—the people who bear His image. Jesus did not say loving our neighbor is a good idea worth trying. It is not an amendment or a recommended add-on to our faith like an extended warranty on a new TV. There is no ambiguity in the Law or Jesus' command. To have a life with God means loving Him and your neighbors.

The link between our vertical relationship to God and our horizontal connection to people is made repeatedly throughout the Scriptures. For example, in Matthew 6:14-15, Jesus said that God's forgiveness of our sins (vertical) depends upon our willingness to forgive others for their sins (horizontal). And in Ephesians 2:13-16, the apostle Paul revealed that Jesus' death on the cross not only reconciled us to God (vertical), but His death has first reconciled us to one another (horizontal). The inseparability of the two is perhaps most boldly stated by John: "If anyone says, 'I love God,' and hates his brother, he is a liar; for he who does not love his brother whom he has seen cannot love God whom he has not seen" (1 John 4:20).

Despite the repeated and clear teaching of Scripture, the two great commandments to love God and others are often uncoupled. It is not uncommon for religious people to cite the first command, "Love God with all your heart," as an excuse for neglecting the second, "and love your neighbor as yourself." Giving God my whole heart, they say, means I cannot give myself in service to others. They believe it requires a monastic separation from the world. Others say it is their love for God that leads them to condemn their neighbors who violate God's law. This was the posture of the Pharisees who opposed Jesus.

This kind of separation and compartmentalization is unnatural to God's character, and it ought to be just as unnatural to ours. Remember how the love shared between the Father, Son and Spirit within the Trinity overflows to us? In the same way, the love, mercy and generosity we experience in communion with our God should also overflow into our relationships with others.

>> Jesus said that our heavenly Father makes His sun shine on the evil and the good, and sends rain on the just and the unjust (see Matthew 5:45). He is generous even to those who do not deserve it. Prayerfully consider whom the Lord is calling you to be generous toward.

Reflection Notes

WHOLE-LIFE GENEROSITY DEVOTIONAL

Day 24 — Generosity Is More than Money

"I have no silver and gold, but what I do have I give to you."
Acts 3:6

IN OUR CULTURE, BOTH INSIDE AND OUTSIDE the church, we tend to limit generosity to financial expression. It's about giving money or economic resources to others. While that is certainly both true and important, this narrow vision of generosity fails to capture its full scope in the Christian's life.

Consider the story of the lame man in Acts 3. Unable to walk from birth, he was deposited at the temple gate every day to beg. Thousands of people would have seen him each day, and yet no one really saw him. This precious child of God was edited out of their minds. He was merely part of the background noise of the city, an unimportant, unnecessary and unseen object of no obvious value.

Then Peter and John came to the temple. We are told that Peter "directed his gaze" at the lame man and so did John. They saw him. He was important to them. Then Peter said to him, "Look at us." After a lifetime of being overlooked and ignored, Peter wanted the beggar to experience the dignity of being seen.

The lame man had been asking for money, but Peter said to him, "I have no silver and gold, but what I do have I give to you. In the name of Jesus Christ of Nazareth, rise up and walk!" The man was immediately healed.

Notice the different forms of generosity Peter and John displayed in the story. First, they offered the man their attention. These two apostles were popular, busy men with rising reputations. Still, unlike the thousands of others who passed the lame beggar each day, Peter and John gave him the dignity of looking him in the eye, of affirming his existence and his value. Then the apostles gave the man restoration. Through Jesus' power, they healed his body.

It is evident that Peter and John were emulating what they had seen Jesus do. Jesus gave of Himself in every way imaginable—His time, attention, love, compassion and power. He even shared His table with sinners and gave up His life for His enemies. Jesus, Peter and John never limited their understanding of generosity to mere silver and gold.

Indeed, Whole-Life Generosity should include the willingness to share our financial resources, but it is about much more than money—it's about all things. This comprehensiveness is captured by Paul in 2 Corinthians 9:8, "And God is able to make all grace abound to you, so that in all things at all times having all that you need you will abound in every good work" (NIV). God has graciously given us all things, and therefore we are called to be gracious in every way.

>> Create a list of ways to be generous beyond giving money. Pray over the list and invite the Spirit to direct your thoughts to a person you may generously bless in one or more of these ways.

Reflection Notes

Day 25 | The Right Way to Play God

Therefore be imitators of God, as beloved children.
And walk in love, as Christ loved us and
gave himself up for us.

Ephesians 5:1-2

WE USUALLY THINK ABOUT "PLAYING GOD" as having a negative connotation. The phrase might be applied to a person who is overly controlling or domineering. Of course, "playing God" is only derogatory if one has a negative vision of God in the first place. When the Apostle Paul tells us to "imitate," or play, God in Ephesians 5, he has something different in mind. He wants us to emulate God's self-giving love.

What follows Paul's command in Ephesians 5 is a list of relationships familiar in the ancient world. Paul writes about husbands and wives, parents and children and slaves and masters. Such lists, known as "household codes," were not limited to the Bible. They were commonplace throughout the Roman Empire where husbands, fathers and masters had absolute authority. What set Paul's household code apart, however, was how he instructed those with power to wield it. Rather than dominating others, as the Romans did, Christians with power were to imitate God by sacrificially loving those under their care. Like Christ who "gave himself up" (Ephesians 5:2, 25), we are also to give ourselves up for others.

In Ephesians 5, Paul is not merely speaking about performing acts of generosity. He is calling us to a fundamentally different posture, a holistic and integrated way of relating to others that seeks their well-being ahead of our own. Whole-Life Generosity, as we've already seen, is not limited to financial giving, and it doesn't happen linearly. It is a virtuous cycle with Jesus at the center. He is both the model and motivator for how we are to serve and bless others.

Following His example, we are to give our lives away for the sake of others. That may sound grandiose, and in some cases it is. There are moments of great heroism that call for a single act of self-sacrifice to save another. These vivid and spectacular acts of generosity are often celebrated, even by non-Christians. Most of us, however, are called to a different form of self-sacrifice. One that is spread out over time. It is the slow, deliberate giving away of our lives so that others might flourish. This kind of love-over-a-lifetime is what Paul wrote about in Ephesians 5. It may be less spectacular, but it is no less divine.

Arthur McGill wrote about this form of self-giving love this way: "To love other people in small but tangible ways over a lifetime is a way of dying. But a slower, drip, drip rather than a big splash. Which is to say that I do think there is something sacrificial and martyr-like in giving small gifts of love to each other. Love is a sacrifice, an expenditure.... The way of Jesus is the way of self-expenditure."

>> How are you called to imitate God in your closest relationships? How would a posture of generosity, of self-giving love, transform the lives of those around you at home and at work?

Reflection Notes

Day 26 | Becoming Kingdom Colonists

*"Your kingdom come, your will be done on earth
as it is in heaven."*
Matthew 6:10

OLIVER WENDELL HOLMES famously observed, "Some people are so heavenly minded that they are no earthly good." This sentiment comes from the mistaken belief that God does not ultimately care about this world, and He's only in the business of rescuing souls off a sinking ship. In the beginning He may have created the heavens and the earth, but some of us act as if the Lord has now retired into full-time church work.

This earth-denying posture is evident when Christians say things like "I'm just passing through on my way to heaven" and "This world is not my home" as if we are mere tourists on planet Earth. Indeed, the Bible does call us "citizens of heaven" (see Philippians 3:20), but citizenship in the ancient world was understood very differently. To be a citizen of Rome, for example, meant you carried the responsibilities of a colonist not a tourist. It was the Roman citizen's duty to transplant the values, customs and structures of Rome wherever they lived. The goal was not to someday escape from Philippi, for example, and return to Rome, but instead to work for the transformation of Philippi into the image of Rome.

So, when Paul referred to Christians as "citizens of heaven," he didn't mean to say we had no responsibilities for this world. In fact, he meant precisely the opposite. It is our responsibility to cultivate the kingdom of heaven right where we are just as our Lord taught us to pray: "Your kingdom come, your will be done on earth as it is in heaven."

There are many ways in which this happens, but one of the most powerful is through the generosity of God's people. As we explored earlier, the world is enslaved by a vision of scarcity. Fearing there isn't enough, citizens of the world fight, cheat, lie, steal and hoard to protect themselves. Citizens of heaven live very differently. They recognize the abundance of God's provision, therefore they are generous to a degree the world often cannot comprehend. And each citizen is generous in different ways and with whatever "currency" the Lord has given them.

Consider the example of the early church in Jerusalem. We are repeatedly told that the believers generously shared their belongings and possessions (Acts 2:45), no one was greedy but shared everything in common (Acts 4:32), there was not a needy person among them (Acts 4:34) and they had "generous hearts" leading them to share their lives, homes and tables (Acts 2:46). These radical expressions of kingdom generosity are possible because citizens of heaven trust in the abundance of God rather than succumb to the scarcity of the earth. And as these foreign but beautiful forms of generosity were seen by others, they were drawn into the kingdom of God as well.

Generosity is often seen as a necessary practice in order to fund the mission of God's kingdom. That is certainly true, but we need to enlarge our vision. Whole-Life Generosity doesn't merely fund God's kingdom; generosity itself is how we display God's kingdom. It is an important way we work together to cultivate heaven right here on earth.

>> In what way does your church or local community of Christians live differently than the surrounding culture? How can you, together, more effectively display the generosity of God's kingdom?

Day 27 From Dutiful to Joyful

Each one must give as he has decided in his heart,
not reluctantly or under compulsion,
for God loves a cheerful giver.
2 Corinthians 9:7

I'VE WONDERED WHETHER MY SON was born with some kind of sixth sense, a sugar radar able to detect when sweets are in the vicinity. When he was four, he approached a group of older women in the park and politely asked for a cookie.

"Why do you think we have cookies?" one of the ladies replied.

"Because you're grandmas. Grandmas always have cookies," he said. He wasn't mistaken. They were grandmothers, they indeed had cookies and my son was rewarded for his charming boldness.

I don't have to tell my son to eat his dessert. Like most kids, as well as adults, he will do that automatically and joyfully. According to scientists this is because our brains are hardwired to crave sugar. Getting him to eat his vegetables— that is a different matter. At best he will eat "green stuff," as he calls it, dutifully. It is merely an obligation imposed on him by his mother and me. (But never his grandmothers. Go figure.)

This is why a recent study from Tufts University caught my attention. Researchers have demonstrated: "It's really possible to rewire people's brains so that they learn to like healthy food and be less tempted by junk food." They've shown that eating vegetables can be transformed from a dutiful chore into a joyful treat through a process they call "cognitive restructuring."

I know, it sounds too good to be true. But it isn't. Real change is possible, and the same is true for generosity.

For many people giving is unnatural. After all, as fearful creatures we are hardwired for self-preservation. That means hoarding our resources to ensure we have enough. That is our sinful default setting. Sacrificial giving is not merely unnatural, it is supernatural. It is the result of God's grace, His power acting in our lives to accomplish what we could never do with our own strength.

At times generosity may be imposed on us as an obligation, like parents forcing children to eat their vegetables. For the Christian, however, this dutiful giving falls short for two reasons. First, we must remember that God does not need our generosity. He is perfectly able to fulfill His goals without our help. So dutiful giving is not a real victory. Second, we are called to reflect the character of God as those created in His image and redeemed to reveal His kingdom. Our heavenly Father does not give reluctantly but joyfully. Jesus even said that giving gives the Father "good pleasure" (Luke 12:32).

Therefore, if we are to be like God, we too should give generously and joyfully. But how? We also need cognitive restructuring, or what Scripture calls the "renewing of our mind" (see Romans 12:2). As we live in intimate communion with God, we will undergo a transformative process in which our minds begin to think more and more like Jesus. We will conform more to His character and His will, and the kind of generosity we once found painful will instead be joyful.

>> Can you identify a way of thinking from your past you no longer hold? What caused you to think differently? As you read the Bible, particularly passages about generosity, invite the Spirit to reveal false beliefs and renew your mind to think like Christ.

Day 28 Opportunity Knocks

And let us not grow weary of doing good, for in due season we will reap, if we do not give up. So then, as we have opportunity, let us do good to everyone, and especially to those who are of the household of faith.
Galatians 6:9-10

WHOLE-LIFE GENEROSITY is rooted in our life with God. As we commune intimately with Him we discover the infinite ways He gives Himself to us. He has blessed us with all things. Our response to this is gratitude. We worship and thank the Lord as His beloved children. Finally, from the overflow of our life with God, we are generous in every way to those around us. In this way we reveal the character of our God and the present reality of His kingdom on earth.

WHOLE-LIFE GENEROSITY CYCLE

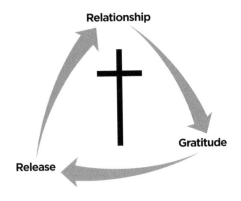

We have come to the end of our four weeks of reflections on living generously. I have one final instruction—pray. Ask God to show you previously hidden opportunities to express His generosity to others. Because Whole-Life Generosity reaches far beyond financial giving, we may not always recognize the countless ways we can give of ourselves to bless others. The opportunities are there; we only lack the eyes to see them. And that's why we must pray.

Paul tells us, "As we have opportunity, let us do good to everyone." In other words, we are to make the most of every opportunity to be generous with our lives, to bless those around us—both believers and nonbelievers. For the last four weeks we've looked at how to awaken and empower Whole-Life Generosity through our communion with God, but to activate that power, we must pray to recognize the opportunities all around us.

I promise that if you ask God to show you ways to be generous to others, He will answer that prayer. "And God is able to make all grace abound in you, so that having all sufficiency in all things at all times, you may abound in every good work" (2 Corinthians 9:8).

>> Commit, individually and as a family or group, to pray each day for opportunities to be generous. When you gather, share these stories and encourage one another to not give up doing good.

Reflection Notes

About the Author

SKYE JETHANI is an award-winning author, speaker, consultant and ordained pastor. He also serves as the co-host of the popular Phil Vischer Podcast, a weekly show than blends astute cultural and theological insights with comical conversation. Skye is the president of Measure the Clouds, a non-profit organization helping a post-Christian generation discover a ravishing vision of life with God. He also leads SkyPilot Media which develops multimedia resources for use by churches, colleges, and community groups navigating the intersection of faith and culture.

He has been a sought-after consultant for groups facing challenges at the intersection of faith and culture, such as the Lausanne Movement, the White House Office of Faith-Based and Neighborhood Partnerships, and the Interfaith Youth Core. He has authored five books and numerous ebooks, and he writes an email-based daily devotional for the smartphone generation called With God Daily.

He lives with his wife, Amanda, and their three children in Wheaton, Illinois.

GenerousChurch equips leaders in churches to unleash whole-life generous disciples. Generosity in Scripture has a much more robust meaning than simply giving money. It is much richer and deeper than we often think and an important key to spiritual formation. Through leadership development, generosity resources, coaching events and other innovative tools, we help church leaders dig deep into the value of Whole-Life Generosity. And through our process, we help these leaders bring new vitality to the church by unleashing generous disciples.

Whole-Life Generosity is an overflowing way of being and living rooted in a vibrant relationship with God that gratefully releases all in love to bless others. It's what God does and it's how we want to live.

Learn more at **www.GenerousChurch.com**

Would you like to share what you've learned with a pastor or church leader?

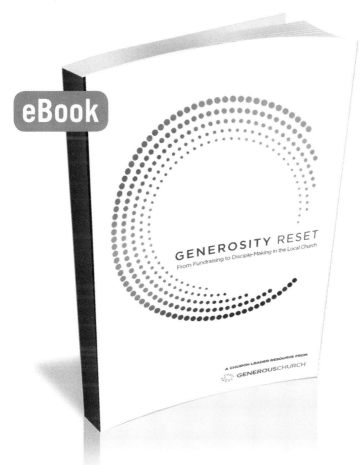

Help us share the Whole-Life Generosity message, and encourage a pastor or church leader to download our complimentary eBook entitled *Generosity Reset: From Fundraising to Disciple-Making in the Local Church.*

Included with the eBook is a free subscription to the *Generosity Reset* videos, a series of six 3-5 minute videos sent to their inbox.

Refer them to **www.GenerousChurch.com/Reset** to subscribe.